CW01512565

Original title:
Radiant Togetherness

Author: Sebastian Sarapuu
ISBN HARDBACK: 978-1-80560-039-8
ISBN PAPERBACK: 978-1-80560-504-1

Shared Sparks of Joy

In laughter bright, we find our place,
Every glance, a warm embrace.
Moments shared, like stars that shine,
Together, hearts and souls align.

In the dance of time, we play,
Chasing clouds that drift away.
Every whisper, a sweet song,
In each other's arms, we belong.

The Symphony of Togetherness

In harmony, our voices blend,
Creating joy that will not end.
Notes of laughter fill the air,
In every moment, love is there.

Melodies of trust entwined,
In every heartbeat, souls aligned.
Together we can rise and soar,
In this symphony, there's so much more.

Blazing Paths Aligned

Through winding trails, we walk as one,
With every step, a challenge won.
In the light of dreams that call,
Together, we can never fall.

With flames of hope, we blaze a way,
Turning night into bright day.
Side by side, our spirits climb,
In unity, we conquer time.

Harmony in Every Glimmer

In the dark, your light will glow,
Guiding me where I need to go.
Every shimmer tells a tale,
In love's embrace, we will not fail.

With every laugh and gentle sigh,
We weave a bond that will not die.
In every glimmer, hope does rise,
Together, we will touch the skies.

Nurtured by Illumination

In the stillness of the night,
A gentle glow does play,
Whispers of the stars above,
Guide our hearts to stay.

Each flicker brings us close,
A bond that never fades,
Bright dreams woven with care,
In love's soft serenades.

Illuminated paths we tread,
With faith as our true guide,
Together we walk onward,
With hope forever wide.

Embraced by warming light,
We find our way anew,
With every step united,
In the magic that we brew.

Nurtured by illumination,
Our souls a radiant dance,
In harmony we flourish,
As we share this sacred chance.

Fusion of Lights

Colors blend and twine,
In twilight's tender hue,
Shadows dance with brilliance,
Whispers of the true.

Stars collide in silence,
Creating cosmic art,
Each spark a story woven,
Of dreams that never part.

A symphony of brightness,
In every gleaming ray,
Together, in this moment,
We seek the light, we play.

Fusion of our spirits,
In radiant embrace,
With every pulse we share,
We fill this sacred space.

Guided by the brilliance,
Of love's enduring fate,
We rise, we shine together,
With hearts forever mate.

Together We Shine

Hand in hand we wander,
Through the paths of the night,
Each step a gentle promise,
Together we ignite.

Dancing 'neath the moonbeams,
Our laughter fills the air,
With every whispered secret,
We're woven without care.

In the glow of friendship,
We find our spirits soar,
A tapestry of moments,
Our hearts forevermore.

Together we are stronger,
As stars begin to gleam,
In unity we flourish,
In every shared dream.

Together we shine brightly,
In love's eternal light,
With joy we face tomorrow,
Our futures burning bright.

Soft Glow of Companionship

In the quiet evening,
A soft glow lingers near,
Warmth found in companionship,
Bringing hearts so near.

The world outside may waver,
But here, we find our peace,
In laughter and in silence,
All worries seem to cease.

Flickering reflections,
In eyes that know the truth,
A gentle coexistence,
Refreshes worn-out youth.

Through storms, we stand together,
In rain or in the sun,
A soft glow of love shines bright,
As life has just begun.

With every heartbeat echoing,
The promise that we share,
A soft glow of companionship,
Is felt beyond compare.

Together in the Gleam

In the quiet of the night, we stand,
Two souls united, hand in hand.
Under stars that brightly gleam,
Together we create a dream.

Whispers carried on the breeze,
Our laughter dances through the trees.
In the warmth of our shared light,
Every moment feels so right.

With each heartbeat, we collide,
In this journey, side by side.
Through shadows, we will find our way,
Together, we greet the day.

Let the sun rise on our fate,
In the bond that will not wait.
As we bask in golden hues,
Together, we will chase the blues.

In the gleam, our spirits soar,
In this life, forevermore.
Each glance holds a spark so true,
Together, just me and you.

Tapestry of Radiance

Woven threads of vibrant hue,
Each moment shared, a stitch anew.
In this tapestry we thread,
With every color, love is spread.

Sunlight dances on the loom,
Creating warmth within the room.
As we craft our shared design,
Threads of fate intertwine.

Every laugh, a pattern spun,
In the glow of the setting sun.
Bound together, rich and bright,
In this dance of radiant light.

Through the fabric of our days,
We create in countless ways.
With each memory, a strand to hold,
In this story, our love unfolds.

A tapestry, forever strong,
In the woven hearts, we belong.
Together in rich array,
In our radiance, we will stay.

The Spirit of Light

In the dawn's embrace, we rise,
Chasing dreams that light the skies.
With every step, shadows fall,
Together, we can have it all.

The spirit whispers soft and clear,
In every word, I feel you near.
With rays of hope and joy in sight,
We dance within the spirit of light.

In the silence, hear the song,
A melody that makes us strong.
With open hearts, we take our flight,
Together, we ignite the night.

As stars align in cosmic grace,
Every heartbeat finds its place.
In this journey, we unite,
Forever in the spirit of light.

Hand in hand, we'll forge ahead,
Guided by the dreams we've fed.
With every dawn, our love ignites,
Together, we are pure delights.

Connected Glow

In the twilight, we find our way,
Connected by the thoughts we say.
Through the glow of evening's fire,
We share in dreams, deep desire.

Every glance ignites a spark,
Illuminating paths through dark.
In the warmth, our hearts will flow,
Together in this connected glow.

As the night unfolds its wings,
We embrace the joy that living brings.
Hand in hand, we mark our path,
Finding wonder in our laugh.

In the quiet of the stars, we linger,
Tracing constellations with our finger.
With every pulse, our love will grow,
Together in this radiant glow.

In moments shared, the world recedes,
We plant love's everlasting seeds.
Boundless hearts in rhythmic tow,
Forever in connected glow.

In Concert with Light

In the dawn's gentle rise,
The world awakens bright,
Colors dance in the skies,
Nature sings with delight.

In whispers of the breeze,
Shadows play with the sun,
A harmony that frees,
Every heart becomes one.

As stars glitter at night,
They weave stories untold,
In the quiet, pure sight,
Dreams and memories unfold.

From mountains high to seas,
The earth hums a soft tune,
In moments like these,
We find our light in the moon.

Together we ignite,
A spark that brightly glows,
In concert with the light,
A bond that ever grows.

The Flame of Companionship

In a warm evening haze,
Friendship fires ignite,
Shared laughter and praise,
Hearts bundled in light.

Through trials we will stand,
The flame will not wane,
Side by side, hand in hand,
Through joy and through pain.

Chasing dreams in the dark,
Together we embrace,
With each whisper, a spark,
We burn brighter in grace.

In every gentle touch,
And the stories we share,
Our spirits, they clutch,
With love beyond compare.

In the shadowy gloom,
Our fire will remain,
The flame of companion's bloom,
A bond that is unchained.

Connection's Glow

In the silence, we find,
A spark that lights the dark,
Words unspoken yet bind,
With an unending mark.

Through the laughter and tears,
We traverse this vast land,
With echoes of our years,
Together we will stand.

In moments grasped so tight,
Time etches our embrace,
Connecting hearts with light,
In this ever-spinning race.

With each glance, we share,
A universe in bloom,
In this dance, a prayer,
Our souls dispel the gloom.

In the bonds that we sow,
A warmth that ever flows,
In the beauty we know,
Is the glow that connection shows.

Gleam of Together

In the dawn's softest glow,
We gather side by side,
Hearts entwined in a flow,
On this beautiful ride.

With laughter we embark,
Dreams twinkling in our eyes,
Finding light in the dark,
Together, we shall rise.

As the seasons unfold,
Our bond will grow more clear,
Each story to be told,
Whispers that draw us near.

In the moments we share,
A tapestry we weave,
With a love that lays bare,
The joy we both believe.

In the gleam that we see,
There's strength in unity,
In this life, you and me,
Together, we will be.

In the Light of Us

In the dawn, we wake anew,
Golden rays, a tender hue.
Hand in hand, we walk the way,
In the light, we find our play.

Every shadow fades from sight,
Together, we ignite the night.
Hope and dreams, we intertwine,
In this glow, our hearts align.

Shared Luminance

Two souls bright, a shared embrace,
In the warmth, we find our place.
Reflections dance in soft delight,
Unified in radiant light.

Threads of joy weave through the air,
In this space, we're free from care.
With each laugh, the world expands,
A tapestry of hearts and hands.

The Force of Connection

When paths converge, the spark ignites,
In silent whispers, magic writes.
Every heartbeat, a gentle call,
Together, we can rise or fall.

Unified, we overcome,
In this dance, our hearts hum.
Bound by trust, we rise and soar,
Through every storm, we seek more.

Light Weaving Hearts

With every thread, we weave the night,
Patterns glimmer, bold and bright.
In the fabric of our dreams,
Love flows softly, or so it seems.

Together, we stitch moments dear,
Crafting joy, erasing fear.
Each stitch a tale, a mark of grace,
In this light, we find our place.

Unity's Warmth

In the heart's embrace we gather,
A tapestry of souls drawn near.
With gentle hands, we weave together,
A bond that whispers, loud and clear.

Through trials faced, we stand as one,
Their strength ignites a brighter flame.
In laughter shared and battles won,
Together we rise, none are the same.

Each voice a note in harmony,
Resounding in an endless song.
In unity, we find our glee,
With open hearts, we all belong.

Like the sun that warms the earth,
We shine as brightly as the day.
In love's embrace, we find our worth,
Together, we will always stay.

In difference, we find our grace,
A world adorned with many hues.
United, we share the same space,
Together, we shall always choose.

Bright Threads of Affection

In gentle whispers, love takes flight,
A fabric woven, strong and bright.
Through every joy and every tear,
We stitch our hearts, forever near.

With laughter's thread, we bind our souls,
Each memory a precious fold.
In every hug, in every smile,
Our bond grows deeper, mile by mile.

Through shadows cast, through storms we brave,
We shine together, bold and brave.
In unity, our spirits sing,
Bright threads of love, in all we bring.

Wrapped in warmth, we walk as one,
Beneath the same, embracing sun.
With every step, we feel the glow,
In life's rich tapestry, we grow.

Together we will make a stand,
With hearts adorned and open hands.
In every moment, rich and true,
Bright threads of love, forever new.

The Dance of Togetherness

Beneath the stars, we take our place,
A sacred rhythm, hearts embrace.
With every step, we find our way,
In harmony, we choose to stay.

The melody of laughter rings,
In every moment, joy it brings.
With each sway, we feel the beat,
Together, life feels more complete.

Through trials faced, we're side by side,
In every challenge, love our guide.
With open arms, we gather near,
In every dance, we shed our fear.

As shadows fade and sunlight shines,
In every twirl, our spirit climbs.
Together we are fierce and free,
The dance of love, our destiny.

In vibrant colors, we will soar,
A symphony that we explore.
With every heartbeat, we expand,
The dance of life, hand in hand.

Harmonized Spirits

In quiet moments, hearts align,
Together weaving trust, divine.
With shared dreams and whispered hopes,
We build a world where love elopes.

Like rivers mingling, strong and free,
Our spirits flow in harmony.
With every word, we lift each other,
In every glance, a deeper tether.

As sun and moon make gentle light,
We balance darkness with the bright.
In unity, we find our grace,
A sacred bond none can erase.

With every laugh, we strengthen ties,
With every tear, our spirits rise.
Connected souls in this vast sphere,
In love's embrace, we have no fear.

So here we stand, hand in hand,
Together strong, together we'll stand.
In every heartbeat, a unified art,
Harmonized spirits, never apart.

Fusion of Bright Spirits

In the twilight's gentle glow,
We gather close, heartbeats echo.
Laughter dances in the air,
With warm embraces, we repair.

Each story shared, a thread so bright,
Binding us in shared delight.
Through trials faced, we find our way,
Together strong, come what may.

In shadows cast, our light won't fade,
As friendships form, foundations laid.
Together we create a spark,
Embracing joy, igniting the dark.

With every smile, a world takes flight,
Transforming gloom into pure light.
In this fusion, spirits rise,
A vibrant dance beneath the skies.

In harmony, we weave our dreams,
In every heart, a brighter beam.
Together, we are bold and free,
A tapestry of unity.

The Beacon of Companionship

In the storms that life can bring,
Our bond becomes a sacred thing.
Through winds of change, we stand our ground,
A lighthouse steady, love unbound.

With every challenge that we face,
Your presence, like a warm embrace.
In laughter shared and tears we find,
The strength to leave our doubts behind.

You light the path, a guiding star,
No distance seems to be too far.
With open hearts, we create a space,
Where dreams take flight, and fears erase.

Through quiet nights and sunny days,
In every moment, our spirits praise.
For in this bond, we find our truth,
A testament to love, our proof.

With you, the world feels so alive,
In every moment, we thrive.
Together, we can face the night,
As beacons of companionship, our light.

Together, We Shine

Underneath the endless sky,
We join our hearts, spirits high.
In gentle whispers, we unite,
Together, we shine, pure and bright.

With every step, we walk as one,
Chasing dreams beneath the sun.
In shared laughter, our worries fade,
In the warmth of love, we're remade.

The world may challenge, life may sway,
But side by side, we'll find our way.
In every shadow, light we'll bring,
Together, oh, how we will sing.

As stars align in cosmic dance,
Our spirits join in sweet romance.
Through every tear, joy, and pain,
Together, we'll dance through the rain.

With open arms and hearts so wide,
In friendship's bond, we take pride.
Together, we light the way,
In every night and every day.

Lighthearted Gatherings

In gardens filled with laughter's sound,
We come together, joy is found.
With every joke and cheerful cheer,
We celebrate the moments dear.

Beneath the sun, our spirits soar,
Each gathering opens a new door.
With playful hearts and minds so bright,
We create memories of pure delight.

In gentle breezes, stories weave,
In every tale, we truly believe.
Together, we craft our own lore,
In the lighthearted times we adore.

With baskets filled and smiles displayed,
Our bonds grow stronger, never fade.
In every hug and playful tease,
We find our joy, we find our peace.

As stars appear to guide the night,
We toast our friendship, hearts alight.
In lighthearted gatherings, we find,
The beauty of souls intertwined.

Starry Alliances

In the quiet of the night,
Stars weave tales up high.
Whispers of the universe,
On dreams they softly lie.

Galaxies collide, they dance,
Across the velvet sky.
Light-years apart, yet near,
In each other's eyes they sigh.

Constellations join as one,
Mapping paths unknown.
In their treasure troves of light,
Hearts find their way home.

Beneath the cosmic blanket,
We share our hopes and fears.
Each twinkle is a promise,
Written through the years.

In this stellar unity,
We're never truly lost.
Together, we create our dreams,
No matter what the cost.

The Embrace of Luminescence

A gentle glow in darkness,
Whispers of the dawn.
Each flicker holds a secret,
A bond that lingers on.

Booming bursts of starlight,
Painting shadows bright.
In the arms of luminescence,
We find our truest sight.

Colors blend in harmony,
As darkness fades away.
In every shade of golden,
We dance until the day.

Moments shared in twilight,
Underneath the moon's grace.
In the warmth of luminescence,
We touch a sacred space.

With every breath, a promise,
To cherish what we find.
In the glow of our embrace,
Love's light remains entwined.

Illuminated Journeys

Upon the winding path we tread,
Lit by the stars above.
Each step unveils a story,
Each journey, fueled by love.

Sunrise spreads its golden hue,
Awakening the ground.
With each dawn, new beginnings,
In sunlight, dreams are found.

The rising tide of evening,
Brings whispers of the sea.
Guided by the moon's soft glow,
We drift, just you and me.

In shadows, we find comfort,
Where light and dark entwine.
Every moment whispers tales,
Of pathways that align.

Together, we explore the light,
In every twist and bend.
Illuminated journeys call,
With love, our hearts transcend.

Harmony in Light

In the light of day we gather,
Voices blend as one.
Together, we sing our stories,
Until the day is done.

With laughter like the sunbeam,
We chase away the gray.
In harmony, we flourish,
Finding joy along the way.

Every shadow tells a story,
Of lessons learned and shared.
In the dance of bright and dark,
Our spirits are laid bare.

As night unfurls its blanket,
We hold each other tight.
In the silence of the stars,
We bask in love's pure light.

Together, we create a symphony,
Of dreams that soar and flight.
In unity, we find our strength,
In the harmony of light.

Bonds of Brilliance

In the quiet night sky,
Stars whisper secrets close,
Together we shine brightly,
A cosmic dance of prose.

Through shadows we will spark,
With laughter lighting up dark,
Each moment, a gem we find,
Like constellations entwined.

In gardens where dreams bloom,
Hearts weave a vibrant loom,
Colors blend, and thoughts align,
In every heartbeat, divine.

From fire to gentle breeze,
We forge our destinies,
In unity, our dreams fly,
Together, we touch the sky.

Through storms and sunny days,
Our bond, the sun's warm rays,
In brilliance, we will stand,
Hand in hand, across this land.

Celestial Harmony

In the silence of the night,
Moonlight dances with delight,
Harmony as soft as breath,
Guides us through the paths of death.

Galaxies turn in embrace,
Rhythms pulse in endless space,
Every heartbeat sings as one,
An ode to what's just begun.

Waves echo through time and space,
Creating a sacred place,
Stars aligned, we hear the call,
Together we shall never fall.

In a universe so vast,
Every moment cannot last,
Yet in love, we find our way,
Through the night, into the day.

Beneath the skies of blue,
Hearts whispered, I love you,
In celestial light we grow,
United in this wondrous glow.

United in Glow

In the twilight's gentle sigh,
Dawn awakens, lifting high,
Hand in hand through the unknown,
In this journey, never alone.

With every step, we ignite,
Passion bursting into light,
In our hearts, a flame we share,
Together, we rise to dare.

Voices blend in sweet refrain,
Echoing through joy and pain,
Guided by the stars above,
We shine bright in endless love.

Each moment woven tight,
A tapestry of pure light,
United in our vibrant hue,
A bond that ever feels so new.

In the depths, we will find,
Reflections of the divine,
In the glow, our spirits soar,
Together forevermore.

The Radiance of Together

In the gleam of dawn's first light,
We hold fast through darkest night,
Side by side, our spirits soar,
The radiance we can't ignore.

Through the trials that we face,
Hope ignites a sacred space,
With each challenge that we meet,
Our connection feels more sweet.

In the whispers of the trees,
Nature sings her soothing pleas,
United in this warm embrace,
We find a heart's resting place.

As the sunsets drape the sky,
We reflect the love that's nigh,
In the colors, bold and bright,
Together, we paint the night.

With each heartbeat, we align,
In this dance, our souls entwine,
The radiance of our tether,
Shines eternally together.

Echoes of Light

In the quiet dusk we find,
Whispers soft, the stars aligned.
Time dances on a silver thread,
Echoes of dreams, a path we tread.

Through shadows cast by fading day,
Light reveals where hearts may stray.
In every spark, a story glows,
A symphony that gently flows.

Beyond the veil, the night will sing,
Of hopes reborn, of fragile wings.
In this embrace, we lift our gaze,
To the horizon's golden blaze.

When twilight fades and silence reigns,
In each heartbeat, love remains.
Echoes of light in every breath,
A testament that conquers death.

We wander on, our souls entwined,
Through realms of ether, unconfined.
In whispers soft, we hear the call,
Of echoes bright that bind us all.

Luminous Affection

In every glance, a flame ignites,
Soft radiance, our shared delights.
Beneath the stars, our spirits soar,
In silent vows, we seek for more.

The night unfolds with tender grace,
In your embrace, I find my place.
Each whispered word, a glowing spark,
A dance of shadows in the dark.

With every pulse, a dream takes flight,
Moments captured, pure and bright.
Through trials faced, our hearts align,
In luminous affection, we shine.

As twilight fades, our souls entwine,
In silver beams, your hand in mine.
Together we weave a tapestry,
Of love and light, eternally.

In every dawn, our hopes renew,
With vibrant hues, a world in view.
A radiant glow that never dims,
In the warmth of us, the universe spins.

The Unity of Stars

In the vastness where silence dwells,
Stars whisper tales that time compels.
A tapestry of shimmering light,
Dances together through the night.

Each twinkle sings of distant dreams,
Of galaxies spun in cosmic schemes.
In unity, their glimmers blaze,
A constellation's timeless praise.

Through darkened skies, their beacon glows,
In every heart, the wonder grows.
For in the night, where shadows play,
We find our way among the stray.

With every blink, a wish is cast,
Connections forged from first to last.
We reach for light, both near and far,
In the unity of every star.

So let us wander, hand in hand,
Through endless skies, across the land.
In every star, a story springs,
A symphony, the universe sings.

Sharing the Flame

In moments quiet, hearts unite,
We gather close, embracing light.
A spark ignites within our cores,
As warmth flows through, forever more.

The fire glows, a gentle beam,
In our laughter, we dare to dream.
With every story shared tonight,
We nurture bonds, igniting bright.

Through whispered words and knowing looks,
In the chapters of our books,
Each flicker holds a memory,
Of perfect peace, of harmony.

As dusk descends, the shadows play,
We hold the flame, come what may.
In unity, our spirits rise,
Together facing the darkened skies.

So let us dance, our hearts aflame,
In this embrace, we'll stake our claim.
For in the warmth of love's sweet call,
We find our strength, we are one, we'll stand tall.

Embracing the Essence

In the whisper of the night, soft and low,
Nature's breath begins to flow.
Stars awake, a dance of light,
Embracing the essence, pure and bright.

Moonbeams weave through the trees,
Carrying secrets on the breeze.
Every shadow tells a tale,
Of love and laughter, the spirit's trail.

Moments linger, as time stands still,
Filling hearts with gentle thrill.
In every pulse, a beat divine,
Embracing the essence, pure and fine.

Soft petals unfurl, bright and bold,
In quiet gardens, stories unfold.
Nature's canvas paints the dawn,
Where every whisper becomes a song.

Together we stand, hand in hand,
In this sacred, timeless land.
Each breath a promise, a fresh start,
Embracing the essence of every heart.

Illuminated Union

Light and shadow waltz in grace,
In the heart's most sacred place.
Fingers intertwined, softly knit,
An illuminated union, a perfect fit.

Underneath the sapphire skies,
Glimmers whisper, never lie.
Together, we dream, daring to soar,
In this bond, we seek for more.

Eyes like lanterns, glow with hope,
Through the darkness, we shall cope.
A spark ignites the unknown,
In this journey, we're not alone.

Time may bend, and seasons shift,
But our union, a timeless gift.
With every heartbeat, stories blend,
Illuminated until the end.

Through laughter's echo and sorrow's tear,
In every moment, you are near.
An illuminated path we trace,
In luminous love's warm embrace.

United by Luminescence

Beneath the stars, we come alive,
In their glow, our spirits thrive.
Every glance a spark, we ignite,
United by luminescence, pure delight.

Dancing shadows play their part,
As light connects each beating heart.
From dusk to dawn, we weave our thread,
A tapestry of words unsaid.

Moments captured in soft embrace,
In the quiet, we find our place.
In every breath, a shared promise,
United by luminescence, endless bliss.

Together we rise, like the sun,
Entwined, two souls have now become one.
With every heartbeat, the night sings,
A love that's boundless, as day springs.

Through storms and calm, we find our way,
In the sun's warm light or moon's soft sway.
Guided by the shine that makes us whole,
United by luminescence, heart and soul.

A Chorus of Glimmers

In the stillness of twilight's haze,
Glimmers gather in soft displays.
A chorus rises, sweet and clear,
Each note a whisper for hearts to hear.

Stars twinkle like a playful crowd,
Celebrating dreams, vibrant and loud.
Together we tune our hearts to sing,
A symphony crafted by love's sweet ring.

Moonlight drapes a silken thread,
Weaving paths where angels tread.
In every glimmer, hope renews,
A beacon bright, guiding our views.

With every laugh, a glimmer's flare,
In moments cherished, beyond compare.
Through valleys deep and mountains high,
A chorus of glimmers fills the sky.

By the firelight, stories flow,
In our shared glow, we'll always know.
Together we'll dance, forever free,
In this chorus of glimmers, you and me.

A Tapestry of Light

Threads of gold and silver gleam,
Woven dreams in sunlight's beam.
Every hue a story told,
In this tapestry of gold.

Whispers dance in radiant grace,
Illuminating every space.
Hearts entwined, a bond so bright,
Together we become the light.

Starlit wishes, shadows fade,
In this magic, unafraid.
Every pulse beats in delight,
Creating warmth, a pure insight.

Colors blend, they intertwine,
Embers spark, our spirits shine.
In every thread, a piece of soul,
In unison, we find our role.

A canvas vast, the world appeals,
With every glance, the heart reveals.
In unity, our strength ignites,
Living art in vibrant lights.

Shining in Unison

Stars above, we reach to gleam,
Glowing together, one bright dream.
Aligned as one, our spirits rise,
In every heart, a thousand skies.

Voices merge, a harmony,
Each note reflects our unity.
In shadows cast, we find our way,
A beacon bright, we will not sway.

Hand in hand, we dance as one,
Embracing warmth, eclipsing sun.
Every smile, a guiding light,
In this together, we take flight.

Moments shared, a treasure vast,
In every echo, futures cast.
Shining brightly, we ignite,
In the darkness, we are light.

Together forged, a sturdy bond,
In every challenge, we respond.
With open hearts, we face each dawn,
Together always, never gone.

The Glow of Togethering

Bright embers of a common heart,
In every rise, we play our part.
A gentle glow embraces all,
In togetherness, we hear the call.

Laughter woven in the night,
In each glance, a spark of light.
Hands together, strong and true,
In every step, we press on through.

Like flowers blooming in the sun,
Together, we are never done.
In every breath, a shared delight,
In this glow, we find our might.

Stars converge in skies of dreams,
Together, stronger than it seems.
A tapestry of souls we weave,
In this bond, we believe.

Journey onward, side by side,
In every moment, joy and pride.
Together we will chart the way,
In this glow, we choose to stay.

Lightweavers

In the quiet, whispers stir,
Weaving tales without a blur.
With gentle hands, we craft the light,
Weaving stories through the night.

Golden threads of joy and peace,
In every stitch, our hearts release.
From dusk till dawn, we intertwine,
Creating dreams that brightly shine.

Together in this sacred space,
We paint the world with love's embrace.
With every color, every tone,
We build a home, no more alone.

With laughter ringing through the air,
No burden too heavy, none to bear.
In each moment, secrets blend,
We are the light, we are the end.

Threads of hope, they never fray,
In every heart, an endless play.
Woven tightly, strong and bright,
As lightweavers, we own the night.

The Light We Share

In shadows deep, we find our way,
With every smile, a light of day.
A spark ignites, a gentle flame,
Together bright, we share the same.

Through storms that rage and winds that howl,
Our bond remains, a steadfast vow.
In quiet nights, the stars align,
The light we share, forever shine.

Through laughter loud and whispers low,
We journey on, through ebb and flow.
In every moment, near or far,
Our hearts alight, a guiding star.

Like fireflies that grace the night,
We dance in circles, pure delight.
With hands entwined, we face our fears,
The light we share will dry our tears.

Together, we weave paths divine,
In every heartbeat, love's design.
With courage bold, we stand, we dare,
Forever strong, the light we share.

Embrace of the Pyre

Beneath the night, the fire glows,
Embers dance as soft wind blows.
We sit as one, hearts intertwined,
In warmth of flames, our souls aligned.

The crackling sound, a soothing song,
In this embrace, we both belong.
The flicker lights your gentle face,
A moment caught, a warm embrace.

With stories shared and laughter bright,
The pyre beckons, igniting night.
In smoky curls, our dreams take flight,
Together bound by love's pure light.

As shadows pass and days unfold,
In memories of warmth, we hold.
The pyre's glow, a timeless trace,
An endless dance, this sacred space.

Through every blaze, our spirits soar,
Embrace of pyre, forevermore.
In hearts afire, our love shall stand,
Together forged, a flame so grand.

The Illumination of Affection

In quiet glances, love ignites,
A soft illumination lights.
Each tender touch, a radiant beam,
In silence shared, we find our dream.

With open hearts, we dare to show,
The warmth within, a gentle glow.
A whispered word, a promise made,
In affection's light, we're unafraid.

Through paths unknown, we walk as one,
With every step, our journey's fun.
The light of us, a guiding force,
In love's embrace, we find our course.

Through trials faced, our love stands tall,
An ornament to crown it all.
In darkest hours, still we shine,
The illumination, love divine.

With every laugh, and every tear,
Our light grows stronger, ever near.
Together we bloom, like flowers fair,
In the illumination of affection, we care.

Threads of Light

In tangled paths, our stories weave,
With every step, our hearts believe.
A tapestry of dreams we thread,
In colors bright, our spirits fled.

The golden rays, the silver gleam,
In every glance, the spark of dream.
With every word, a strand we share,
In woven love, beyond compare.

Through trials faced and joys embraced,
These threads of light, we have encased.
With every laugh and every sigh,
We build a world where love won't die.

In darkest nights, we still will shine,
Our threads entwined, forever divine.
With hope as bold as stars above,
We stitch our fate, in endless love.

Together strong, with every fight,
We stand as one, in threads of light.
A vibrant quilt, our lives entwined,
In love's embrace, true peace we find.

Illuminated Bonds

In shadows cast, we find our way,
A guiding light to share today.
With every heartbeat, strength we share,
Illuminated bonds, beyond compare.

Through trials faced, our spirits rise,
Together we soar, touch the skies.
Hands entwined as one, we stand,
Illuminated hearts, a fearless band.

In laughter bright, our joy ignites,
Through darkest paths, we find our sights.
With whispers soft, we speak our truth,
In the glow of love, reclaim our youth.

No distance vast can break this chain,
In unity's warmth, we feel no pain.
Each flicker fuels the fire within,
Illuminated bonds, we all begin.

So let the stars above align,
In this sacred space, your heart is mine.
Together we create, so brave, so bold,
Illuminated bonds, a tale retold.

Harmony's Embrace

In twilight's glow, we gently sway,
In melody's arms, we lose our way.
Each note a promise, softly spun,
Harmony's embrace, where love has won.

We dance as one, with grace unbound,
In every heartbeat, a soothing sound.
With every breath, a symphony,
Harmony's embrace, you and me.

Underneath the stars, we find our peace,
In whispered dreams, we find release.
With fingers laced, we traverse time,
Harmony's embrace, a sweetened rhyme.

Through storms that rage, we hold so tight,
In shadows deep, we seek the light.
Together we weave a tale so grand,
Harmony's embrace, hand in hand.

Forever bound in this gentle flow,
In unity's warmth, our spirits glow.
Embraced by love, we rise above,
Harmony's embrace, a gift from love.

Luminous Connections

Across the skies, our dreams take flight,
In every heart, a spark ignites.
With open eyes, the world we see,
Luminous connections, you and me.

In every laugh, a shared delight,
In whispers soft, we chase the night.
Together we wander, explore the divine,
Luminous connections, forever shine.

Through valleys low and mountains high,
In every moment, we learn to fly.
With every heartbeat, rhythms align,
Luminous connections, truly divine.

In echoes of joy, our spirits sing,
In depths of silence, love's offering.
Bound by light, our souls entwined,
Luminous connections, so well defined.

So let us gather, hearts ablaze,
In this bright dance, we'll always praise.
With open arms, we'll face the sun,
Luminous connections, we are one.

United in Light

In the dawn's glow, we find our way,
With voices strong, we seize the day.
Together we rise, side by side,
United in light, hearts open wide.

Through darkest nights, our hope remains,
In every struggle, love sustains.
With courage deep, we face the fight,
United in light, we shine so bright.

In every tear, a lesson learned,
From every challenge, our spirits turned.
We lift each other, hearts in flight,
United in light, our souls ignited.

Together we stand, through thick and thin,
In every loss, we will begin.
With hands held tight, we bless the night,
United in light, forever right.

So let the stars our path adorn,
In every dawn, a new day born.
Embraced by hope, we hold on tight,
United in light, our hearts alight.

The Glow of Shared Dreams

In twilight hues our visions blend,
With whispered hopes, our hearts ascend.
Through starlit paths, we find the way,
Together bright, we greet the day.

Each laugh a spark, each tear a thread,
In kindred souls, our fears are shed.
As dreams entwine like vines that grow,
We nurture light, let love bestow.

The horizon calls, a dawn so near,
With faith and trust, we cast out fear.
In unity our futures gleam,
A world alive, a vibrant dream.

Hand in hand, we face the night,
With every step, we feel the light.
In shared embraces, warmth surrounds,
Through every challenge, hope abounds.

Our journey weaves a song so sweet,
In every heartbeat, rhythms meet.
The glow persists, forever bright,
In shared dreams, we find our light.

Shimmering Unity

In a world of colors, side by side,
We dance together, hearts open wide.
Each moment whispers, soft and clear,
In shimmering unity, all is near.

With laughter echoing through the air,
We'll face the storms, we'll stand and care.
Our hands connect like threads of gold,
A bond unbroken, forever bold.

Through shadows deep, we stand our ground,
In every silence, love is found.
A spark ignites, igniting flames,
In unity, we feel no shame.

Together we rise, like dawn's embrace,
Every heartbeat finds its place.
In shimmering light, our spirits soar,
In this sacred space, we want no more.

The tapestry of life is ours to weave,
With every thread, we believe.
In shimmering unity, we shine bright,
Guiding each other through the night.

Illuminated Connections

In crowded rooms, our eyes do meet,
A silent bond, both strong and sweet.
Through words unspoken, hearts align,
In illuminated connections, we intertwine.

With every glance, the stories flow,
Of journeys shared, of highs and lows.
Together we laugh, together we cry,
In every heartbeat, time flies by.

Through every trial, we learn and grow,
With trust and love, our spirits glow.
Our paths converge like rivers wide,
Creating currents where dreams can glide.

From fleeting moments to lasting ties,
Each connection shines, a brilliant prize.
In illuminated visions, we embark,
Carving our names upon the dark.

As stars emerge in the evening sky,
We find our place, together we fly.
In this vast world, our hearts connect,
In illuminated ways, we reflect.

A Tapestry of Warmth

In gentle threads, our stories weave,
A tapestry of warmth we believe.
With colors bright, each tale unfolds,
In moments shared, our lives are told.

Through laughter's echo, through whispers low,
The fabric grows, with each hello.
In every hug, in every smile,
We stitch together, mile by mile.

The warmth of kinship, a radiant glow,
In crowded hearts, we freely sow.
With kindness wrapped in every seam,
A tapestry rich, a cherished dream.

Through storms and sun, we hold so tight,
In every challenge, we find our light.
Together, forever, hand in hand,
In this warm embrace, we take our stand.

As seasons change, our bond stays strong,
In this tapestry, we all belong.
With love as the thread, we'll never part,
In a tapestry of warmth, we share our heart.

Brilliance in Unity

In harmony we stand tall,
Voices lift, we heed the call.
Together strong, we rise each day,
In unity, we find our way.

Hands entwined, we move as one,
With every battle, we have won.
Shining brighter, hearts ablaze,
In brilliance, we embrace our days.

Through storms that test, we hold the line,
In every struggle, love will shine.
With every step, we weave a thread,
In unity, our fears are shed.

A tapestry of hopes we weave,
In every heart, a dream we leave.
Together, let our spirits soar,
For in this bond, we are much more.

With laughter shared and tears that blend,
Each moment cherished, we transcend.
In love's embrace, we find our might,
Together, we are pure delight.

The Glow of Kinship

A gentle light in every heart,
In kinship's bond, we play our part.
Through shadows cast, we find a way,
In love's embrace, we choose to stay.

The glow of souls, a guiding flame,
In every joy, we share the same.
Through trials faced, we lift each other,
In every laugh, we see a mother.

With every hug, warmth's sweet delight,
In laughter's echo, hearts take flight.
We walk this path, hand in hand,
In kinship's glow, our spirits stand.

Beneath the stars that shine above,
We weave a story, pure as love.
In every tear that we embrace,
In kinship's glow, we find our place.

For every moment shared in time,
In joyful hurt, we find our rhyme.
A bond unbroken, fierce and bright,
In the glow of kinship, we unite.

In Each Other's Light

When shadows fall and hope feels thin,
In each other's light, we begin.
With hearts ablaze, we face the night,
Together shining, bold and bright.

Through whispered dreams, we build a bridge,
In every smile, a loving wedge.
With hands so warm, we cross the dark,
In each other's light, we find our spark.

With laughter sweet, our spirits blend,
In joy and sorrow, we transcend.
Through every storm, our hearts align,
In unified strength, our souls entwine.

With gentle words, we light the way,
In every dawn, we greet the day.
Through trials faced, we draw on love,
In each other's light, we rise above.

With every breath, we forge anew,
In radiant bonds, we find our crew.
In moments shared, our futures shine,
In each other's light, love is divine.

Celestial Companionship

Beneath the stars, we find our home,
In cosmic dance, we freely roam.
With every dream, our hearts collide,
In celestial bonds, we take our ride.

Through galaxies, our spirits soar,
In friendship's light, we seek for more.
With every laugh, a spark ignites,
In companionship, we reach new heights.

Among the planets, we share our fate,
In each encounter, we cultivate.
Together forged in stardust bright,
In celestial warmth, we find our light.

With every whisper of the night,
In cosmic love, we take our flight.
Through all the chaos, we remain,
In celestial harmony, we gain.

As meteors streak across the sky,
In every moment, we learn to fly.
Bound by the stars that guide our way,
In celestial companionship, we stay.

Rays of Together

In the morning light we rise,
Bound by laughter, no disguise.
Sharing secrets, dreams to weave,
In this bond, we all believe.

With every challenge that we face,
Hand in hand, we find our place.
Together strong, we stand as one,
Chasing shadows, seeking sun.

Through the storms that may arise,
We find shelter, in each other's eyes.
Spreading warmth, igniting hope,
In this journey, we learn to cope.

Moments captured, time we share,
Memories linger in the air.
With every heartbeat, we ignite,
The rays of love, a guiding light.

So here's to us, forever true,
In this world, just me and you.
In the silence, hear our song,
Together is where we belong.

Light in Community

In the heart of every street,
Kindness blooms, where strangers meet.
Voices mingling, joy displayed,
A tapestry, lovingly made.

Through every whisper, every cheer,
Together, we conquer fear.
A shared vision, dreams alive,
In unity, we learn to thrive.

Hands are reaching, hearts embraced,
In this bond, no time is wasted.
Side by side, we pave the way,
Lighting paths, come what may.

In our stories, we find grace,
With every smile, a warm embrace.
Together we rise, never apart,
A shining light, in every heart.

So let us gather, voices strong,
In this community, we belong.
With every step, we'll walk as one,
A journey shared, a race well run.

Embers of Unity

In the silence of the night,
Embers glow, warm and bright.
Together, in shadows, we stand,
United souls, hand in hand.

Through the trials that we face,
We find comfort, find our place.
With each spark, a story told,
In unity, we break the cold.

With whispered dreams, our hopes align,
Bound by love, a sacred sign.
In every heart, the fire grows,
Together, stronger; this we know.

As the evening stars appear,
We gather close, holding dear.
Through the dark, we'll light the flame,
For in unity, we are the same.

So let the embers gently spark,
In this world, we'll make our mark.
With every heartbeat, standing tall,
Together we rise, we will not fall.

The Warmth of Togethering

In the morning's gentle embrace,
We find solace in this space.
With laughter shared and stories spun,
The warmth of hearts, we have begun.

Through the changing of the tide,
We gather close, side by side.
Every moment, a treasure shared,
In this love, we are prepared.

Like a fire that brightly glows,
Together's warmth is all that shows.
In the quiet and the loud,
In unity, we're always proud.

Echoes of dreams fill the air,
Strength in numbers, love to share.
With open arms and joyful eyes,
The warmth of togethering never dies.

So let us dance in the glow of light,
In this together, we feel so right.
Through every season, every weather,
In love's embrace, we stand together.

Glow of Friendship

In the warmth of laughter, we find our way,
Through shared moments, brightening the day.
Hand in hand, we journey along,
In the glow of friendship, we are strong.

Every secret whispered, a bond so tight,
Together we shine, a guiding light.
In every shadow, we seek the sun,
In the glow of friendship, we are one.

Through storms and trials, we stand so near,
With hearts united, we conquer fear.
The glow of trust in every glance,
In the dance of friendship, we take a chance.

With every memory, our spirits grow,
In the garden of laughter, our love will flow.
In the glow of friendship, we find our peace,
A bond unbroken, may it never cease.

As stars above in the darkest night,
Friendship's glow, a beautiful sight.
Together we celebrate, joy on the rise,
In the hearts we cherish, true love lies.

Illuminated Hearts

In a world draped in twilight's embrace,
Illuminated hearts gather in grace.
Soft whispers of kindness, a gentle start,
Lighting the path to each other's heart.

With every story shared, the light expands,
United by dreams that life commands.
In the glow of hope, we find our song,
Illuminated hearts, where we belong.

Casting shadows aside, we reach for the stars,
In the warmth of friendship, we heal our scars.
With each shared laughter, the night feels bright,
In the dance of our spirits, hearts take flight.

Beneath the moon's gaze, we gather tight,
Illuminated hearts, a beautiful sight.
Together we stand, facing life's tide,
In the glow of love, forever our guide.

In the tapestry of life, threads interlace,
With illuminated hearts, we weave our grace.
Through trials and triumphs, we boldly depart,
In the journey of souls, we never part.

Intertwined Illuminations

In a canvas of dreams, colors blend true,
Intertwined illuminations in me and you.
Through the laughter of days, our spirits unite,
In the warmth of connection, we ignite.

With every moment shared, the bond grows strong,
Illuminated paths where we both belong.
Hand in hand, we traverse the night,
Through intertwined illuminations, we find our light.

The echoes of joy in our hearts resound,
In the silence of sharing, love is found.
Together we rise, shining so bright,
In the dance of our souls, we reach new heights.

With each tender glance, our spirits align,
In the embrace of friendship, our love will shine.
Intertwined illuminations, a beautiful view,
In the tapestry of life, forever true.

With the stars as our guide, we journey on,
Creating memories from dusk till dawn.
In a world full of hope, we make our mark,
Intertwined illuminations, bright in the dark.

Collective Spark

In the heart of togetherness, we find our flame,
A collective spark that knows no name.
Through shared visions and dreams that inspire,
We gather our thoughts, fueling desire.

Each voice a note in the symphony's song,
Together we rise, where we all belong.
In the dance of our spirits, we create the art,
With every shared moment, we play our part.

In unity's embrace, we shine even brighter,
Each heart a beacon, a diligent fighter.
With laughter and dreams, we light up the dark,
In this collective spark, we leave our mark.

Through valleys of struggle, we stand as one,
With hope as our guide, we shine like the sun.
In the depth of our love, we find the truth,
A collective spark, the essence of youth.

So let us gather, ignite, and inspire,
With hearts aligned, setting the world afire.
Together we rise, in harmony's arc,
In the journey of life, hold tight to our spark.

Glow of Togetherness

In the dusk, we find our light,
Two souls dancing in the night.
Whispers soft, like a gentle breeze,
Together, we sway with such ease.

Hand in hand, through shadows we tread,
Paint the world in hues of red.
Laughter echoes, sweet and bright,
In this glow, everything feels right.

Side by side, we dream and soar,
Our hearts united, forevermore.
In the silence, our souls align,
In this journey, you are mine.

Through the storms and sunny days,
Together, we find endless ways.
With each moment, our spirits rise,
A shared glow beneath the skies.

And when night falls, and stars appear,
Your presence is what I hold dear.
In the warmth of your embrace,
I find my forever place.

Sparkling Souls

Two spirits twinkling, side by side,
In a world where dreams collide.
With every laugh, a story's spun,
Our journey together has just begun.

In your eyes, a galaxy shines,
Every moment, love redefines.
With spark and fire, our hearts unite,
In the darkest, we find our light.

Hand in hand, we chase the dawn,
In the dance of life, we are drawn.
From whispered wishes to bold designs,
In this tapestry, our love combines.

Through every trial, our spirits soar,
Together, forever, we'll explore.
Each heartbeat sings a sweet refrain,
In this harmony, love's our gain.

With every glance, the spark ignites,
Filling the world with pure delights.
Together we shine, in joy, we pool,
Bound forever, sparkling souls.

The Symphony of Us

In a world alive with fragile sounds,
We play a tune where love abounds.
Every note, a heartbeat's dance,
Together, we find our chance.

With every rhythm, our spirits blend,
In this harmony that won't end.
Sweet melodies in the starlit night,
Our symphony feels so right.

Two voices rise, a perfect blend,
In this song, our hearts transcend.
Each lyric whispers tales untold,
Of a love that never grows old.

Through crescendos and soft refrains,
In this music, we have no chains.
Together, we've forged our own tune,
In the silence, under the moon.

So let the world sing our song loud,
In every crowd, stand out proud.
For in this symphony, we are free,
The melody of you and me.

Shimmering Hearts

In twilight's glow, our hearts collide,
A dance of dreams where love won't hide.
With each heartbeat, a spark ignites,
Together, we scale the heights.

The moonlight kisses our tender sighs,
In this moment, love never lies.
With shimmering glances, sweet and pure,
In your embrace, I find my cure.

Through every challenge, hand in hand,
Together we rise, together we stand.
In the glow of love, we take flight,
Shimmering hearts, a beautiful sight.

With laughter ringing in the air,
Every word spoken, a loving prayer.
In the depths of night, our spirits soar,
In this love, we crave for more.

So let us cherish this shining bond,
In every heartbeat, we respond.
With shimmering hearts, forever we'll be,
In this love, we're wild and free.

Lightwoven Souls

In the tapestry of night, stars gleam,
Threads of silver, woven dreams.
Hearts entwined, a radiant bond,
Guided by light, forever fond.

Whispers echo through time and space,
In every shadow, we find grace.
Souls igniting, flames that soar,
Together we shine, forevermore.

Dancing softly, in twilight's glow,
Sharing secrets only we know.
With every heartbeat, we ignite,
Love's brilliance, a guiding light.

Boundless journeys, we embark,
With every spark, we leave our mark.
In the vast expanse, we prevail,
Lightwoven souls, we will not fail.

Through trials faced, hand in hand,
We'll write our stories in the sand.
With light as armor, love as guide,
Together forever, side by side.

United in Brilliance

Beneath the sky, where colors collide,
We stand as one, with hearts open wide.
A chorus of voices, melodies blend,
Together in laughter, on each other depend.

Radiant rays of hope we share,
In this vibrant journey, love fills the air.
With each moment, our spirits entwine,
In a dance of brilliance, so divine.

Every challenge a spark ignites,
Guiding us through the darkest nights.
Together we rise, through storm and mist,
In unity's glow, our dreams persist.

With every heartbeat, we resonate,
Creating a world where love won't wait.
United in brilliance, we'll pave the way,
Hand in hand, come what may.

A lighthouse shining, steadfast and true,
Guiding lost souls, welcoming you.
In this haven of light, we stake our claim,
Embracing our truth, igniting the flame.

Celestial Embrace

Under the canopy of the endless night,
Stars whisper secrets wrapped in light.
In the celestial embrace, we find peace,
A moment of stillness, a sweet release.

Galaxies twirl in a dance of fate,
Boundless wonders, we meditate.
In dreams of stardust, hearts collide,
In the universe's arms, we abide.

With every breath, we feel the spark,
Infinite connections that leave a mark.
Through cosmic winds, our spirits soar,
A celestial embrace, forevermore.

In the silence, we hear the call,
Echoes of love, enriching us all.
Wrapped in warmth, like the sun's embrace,
In this radiant glow, we find our place.

Every heartbeat, a cosmic rhyme,
In this grand dance, transcending time.
Together we shine, like stars alight,
In the celestial embrace, our spirits take flight.

Flourishing in Luminescence

In gardens of light, love blooms anew,
Every petal glistens in morning dew.
Under the sun's warm, golden gaze,
We flourish in luminescence, a vibrant phase.

With roots intertwined, we stand tall,
Through seasons of change, we embrace all.
In the dance of shadows and brilliant rays,
We celebrate life in countless ways.

Every challenge a chance to grow,
In unity, our strength will glow.
Together we rise, like flowers in spring,
In this garden of dreams, our hearts take wing.

Guided by hope, we chase the dawn,
In the light of love, fears are gone.
Flourishing brightly, side by side,
In luminescence, our souls abide.

With every heartbeat, we spread our wings,
In this radiant space, our joy sings.
Together we bloom, in passion's embrace,
Flourishing in luminescence, a sacred space.

The Warmth of Belonging

In the heart where love does bloom,
Laughter dances, chasing gloom.
Together we build, side by side,
In this place, our spirits glide.

Friendship weaves a sacred thread,
Embracing dreams, where hope is spread.
With every heartbeat, joy ignites,
In our unity, future delights.

Shared stories echo through the night,
Guiding us with soft, warm light.
In the safe harbor, we find peace,
Our bonds grow strong, never to cease.

Through storms and trials, we will stand,
Hand in hand, a steadfast band.
In this warmth, we truly thrive,
In the love we share, we are alive.

From every joy and all despair,
Together, burdens we shall share.
In this haven, we belong,
In our hearts, we sing our song.

Kinship in Radiance

When twilight falls, we gather near,
A circle bright, with hearts sincere.
Laughter sparkles in the stars,
Together, we know no bars.

In every glance, a story told,
With hands entwined, we break the mold.
Through gentle whispers, spirits soar,
Weaving dreams forevermore.

Sunrise brings a golden hue,
Every moment, fresh and true.
In this kinship, joy ignites,
Shining brightly, our shared lights.

Together we face what may come,
In unity, we find our home.
Through every shadow, we will stand,
Together, heart in heart, hand in hand.

In this bond, our spirits thrive,
In radiant love, we're truly alive.
Kinship dances in the night,
Illuminated by friendship's light.

Sparkling Journeys Together

With every step, new paths unfold,
Adventures shared, memories bold.
Through valleys deep and mountains high,
Together, we reach for the sky.

The road is long, but we won't tire,
With laughter's spark, we fuel the fire.
In every twist, a story we write,
In our journey, hearts feel light.

From dawn's first glow to evening's fall,
We chase the dreams that beckon us all.
Every moment, a treasure near,
In the tapestry of love, we steer.

Through every storm and gentle breeze,
We find our way with playful ease.
Hand in hand, through time we roam,
In every heart, we find our home.

In sparkling tales of joy we weave,
Together, we dare to dream and believe.
With open hearts, the world awaits,
On this journey, love creates.

A Chorus of Light

In harmony, our voices rise,
Like morning sun in endless skies.
Together we sing, hearts aligned,
In every note, our dreams combined.

Through the silence, melodies soar,
Echoing love forevermore.
With each refrain, our spirits dance,
Inviting all to share the chance.

In moments shared, we find our sound,
Together, joy is always found.
Our laughter rings, a sweet embrace,
In this chorus, we find our place.

The music swells as stars appear,
In unison, we cast out fear.
With grateful hearts, we stand so tall,
As one, we answer love's sweet call.

In the symphony of life we share,
Each heartbeat sings, a gentle prayer.
In this duet, we rise above,
A chorus of light, wrapped in love.

Kinship in the Glow

In the quiet evening light,
Laughter floats on the breeze,
Hands link in a gentle bond,
Hearts warm as shadows seize.

Stories woven through the air,
Whispers shared, secrets told,
In the glow of kinship's care,
A tapestry of hearts unfold.

Eyes glisten with memories bright,
Each moment a precious thread,
Together we face the night,
With love as our woven bed.

From laughter's spark to quiet sigh,
Bonds deepen as shadows roam,
In the glow, we learn to fly,
Finding in each other home.

When storms of life try to fray,
We stand strong, hand in hand,
In kinship's glow, we find our way,
United, forever we stand.

Kindred Illuminations

In the night, stars align,
Kindred spirits shine so bright,
Casting warmth on every heart,
Filling darkness with soft light.

Through laughter and shared delight,
We dance under the velvet sky,
Each moment a treasured spark,
Every glance, a soft sigh.

Together we navigate dreams,
Illuminations from the soul,
In the tapestry of our beams,
We find truth that makes us whole.

No shadows can dim our flame,
In unity, we rise and play,
With each kindred name we claim,
Love's light guides us on our way.

In this bond, we find our grace,
Hand in hand, forever we roam,
For in kindred's warm embrace,
We weave our stories, our home.

Harmony's Glimmer

Soft notes in the evening air,
Echoes of laughter and song,
In harmony, we find our way,
Together, where we belong.

In the dusk, our shadows blend,
Colors merging in gentle flight,
With every heartbeat, we ascend,
A symphony in the night.

The stars above twinkle bright,
Reflecting the bond we share,
In harmony, hearts take flight,
Each gentle whisper a prayer.

As moonlight bathes the earth,
We find peace in each embrace,
In this moment, knowing worth,
Together, we fill the space.

With every glance, hope ignites,
In the rhythm of love's glow,
Our souls dance in joyful lights,
In harmony's sweet, soft flow.

Interwoven Luminescence

Threads of light in twilight weave,
A canvas bright with love's embrace,
Every moment, we believe,
In the warmth of our shared space.

In laughter's echo, we find peace,
Joy sparkles in the quiet night,
With each shared glance, troubles cease,
Together, our spirits take flight.

The soft glow of kinship shines,
Painting paths we dare to tread,
In every heartbeat, a sign,
Interwoven, where love is bred.

As we navigate life's vast sea,
Our hearts beat in perfect tune,
In this dance, we're wild and free,
Beneath the watchful moon.

In every dream that we embrace,
Luminous tales will create,
Interwoven, a timeless grace,
Together, we illuminate fate.

www.ingramcontent.com/pod-product-compliance
Ingram Content Group UK Ltd.
Pitfield, Milton Keynes, MK11 3LW, UK
UKHW021440290125
4349UKWH00039B/562

9 781805 605041